HOW TO:
DEVELOP EMOTIONAL INTELLIGENCE AND RESILIENCE

BY
DR VEENA V NANJANGUD
VN9 CLINICAL SERVICES LTD

AUTHOR:

Dr Veena V Nanjangud
MBBS
Postgraduate Diploma in Business Administration (Open)

Managing Director
VN9 Clinical Services Ltd
Career, Business & Life Coaching
Publishing in Medical & Healthcare
Business & Management Consultancy
Health Coaching Podcasts

@VN9ClinicalS
VN9ClinicalS.com

© Veena Nanjangud
2024

PROLOGUE

Emotional Intelligence (EI), Emotional Quotient (EQ): These terms are used to describe and define the way we react, behave and respond to circumstances and in the face of adversities. This mini-book gives an instructional guide to developing emotional intelligence and resilience. It includes coaching worksheets that one may use to get a better outlook and deeper understanding of the soft skills necessary to survive and thrive in today's fast paced and competitive world.

1.
EMOTIONAL INTELLIGENCE

"TRUE DEVOTION TO ONE'S WORK IS NON-COMPETITIVE"

Emotional intelligence gives us a greater awareness and recognition of our emotions and helps manage relationships. It consists of the following aspects:

Self Awareness
Self Management
Social Awareness
Relationships management

Self awareness:

Self awareness develops from thinking about and reflecting on past events, awareness of feelings and response to those events that led to the behaviour. Developing the self-awareness facet of emotional intelligence can help improve focus, modify behaviour to achieve a different response to the same triggering event, and find flow.

Flow is the term given to a focused and deep state of work when it is easily done without any interruptions. Developing self awareness helps in achieving concentration towards a deeper flow of focused work, that can greatly improve productivity.

Self management:

Managing self comprises recognising the circumstances and contemplating the next best ways to action. It also includes taking into account different points of view with new & different perspectives to arrive at decisions effectively.

Self management is when you take a moment to calm down before reacting to situations and circumstances.

Things such as mindful breathing for a few minutes, relaxation activities such as listening to music, and making time for getting different perspectives before coming to conclusions help slow the reaction times.

Social awareness:

Social awareness is about noticing what's happening with other people in social circumstances. It consists of being aware of one's senses and intuition, and how comfortable are you around others, in social situations. Being socially aware involves practising mindfulness to be in the moment. Having social awareness and appreciating what the other person is going through with empathy helps with improving relationships.

Relationships management:

Managing relationships starts with developing your strengths and being genuine and authentic. Recognise what your strengths are in social situations and the effects of personalities and personal styles. Seek feedback from trusted people and refine to achieve small wins. Effective communication with others by focusing on the perceived message that others comprehend helps, rather than what is spoken.

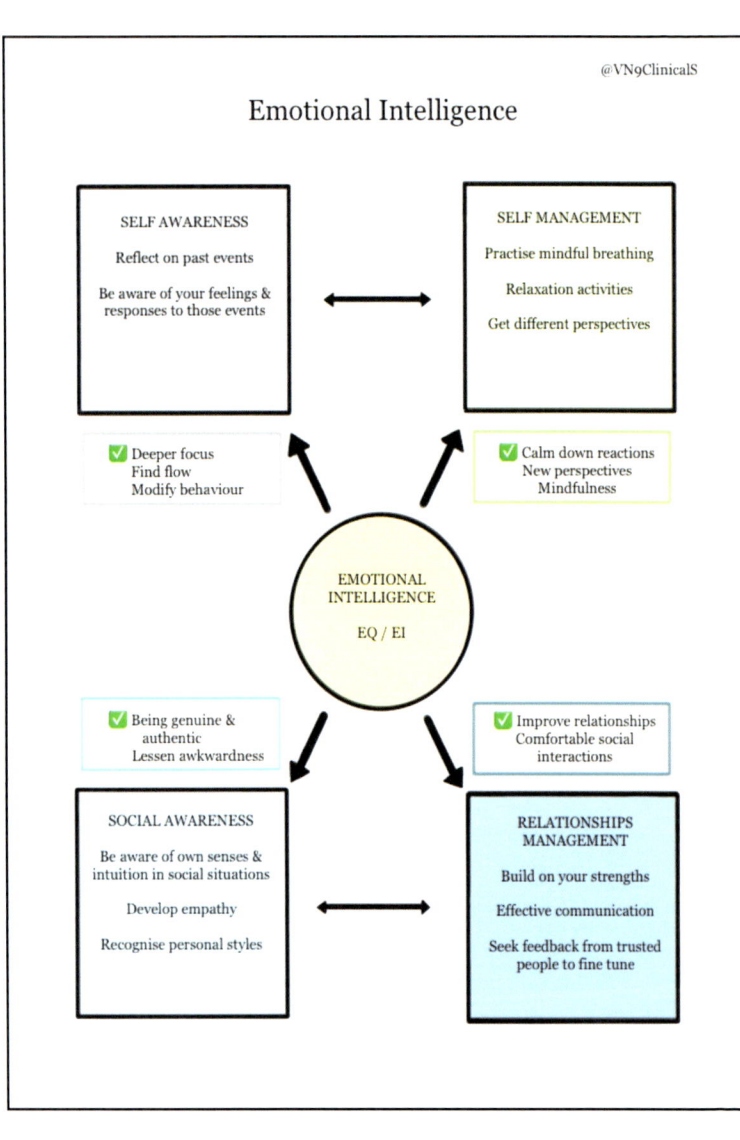

2.
MINDSET COACHING

"PHILOSOPHY OF LIFE INFLUENCES MORE THAN ANYTHING ELSE"

When we look at attitudes, coach-ability and psychological mindedness are the keys to opening the door to the mindset. Attitudes, mindsets and philosophies of life influence the way we think and behave. Coach-ability determines how open one is, to realise that their outlook towards problems in life, may be inflated and overvalued.

What people think the problem is, may be perceived as huge and ballooned as compared to what the problem really is.

Attitudes and mindsets also tend to influence how kind people are towards themselves when faced with difficult circumstances. Placing a hand over one's heart and affirmations that "you have got this" with self-kindness in facing the various and maybe unexpected obstacles in life, helps in decreasing anxieties and stress levels.

3.
ROLES

"LIFE OFTEN FOLLOWS THE CHARACTERS OF ITS MOTIVES"

Recognising roles can make one transact more effectively towards the expectations of others in personal, professional and societal situations.

Awareness and recognition of roles can happen when one pauses and reflects. The three settings of personal, professional and social roles that a person interacts with on a daily basis, can intertwine and interfere greatly.

That's when one contemplates,

Is there any role confusion.. Am I being expected too much from this role.. Is there any mismatch between the roles?

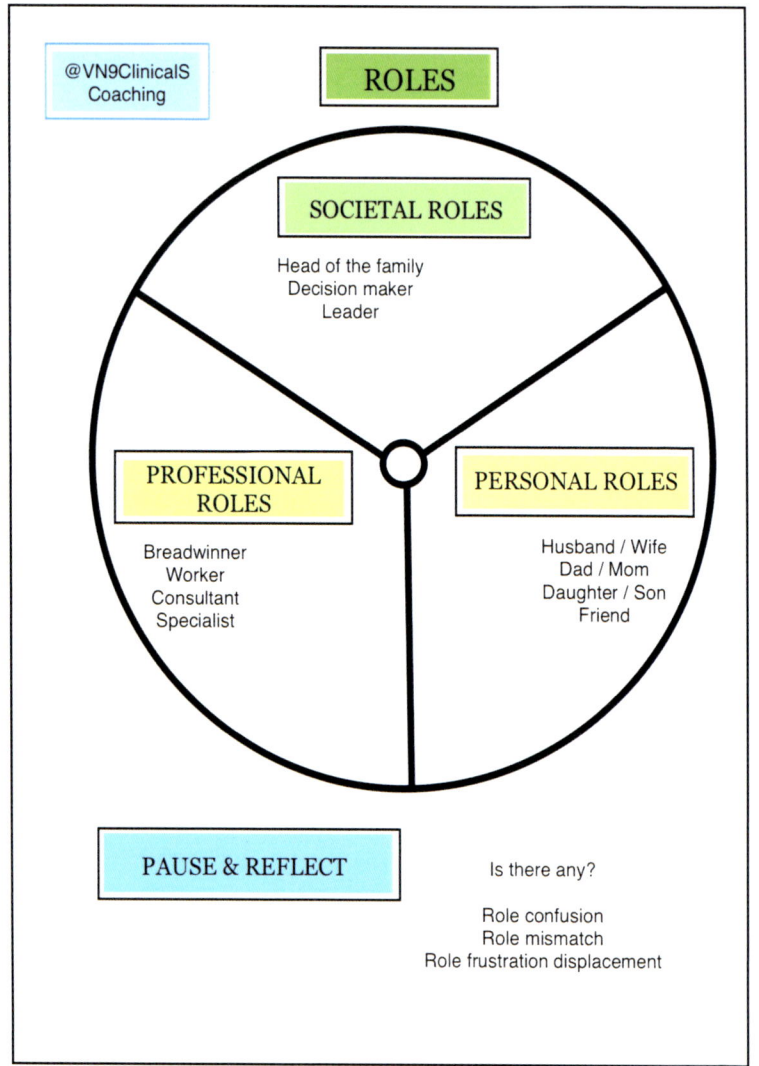

Role frustration displacement is a common cause of many irritations and arguments. For example, one may take out the stresses and irritability of office work at home and with family, with role frustration displacement of professional role problems shown towards personal roles.

4.
PATIENCE

"GOOD THINGS TAKE TIME"

Lack of patience is the root cause of many problems, frustrations and irritations in life. The developing patience coaching activity worksheet gives ways to remain calm and practice patience. Role frustration displacement can come across as impatience. The physical effects of impatience can cause anger rush, clenched jaws, anxiety and irrational behaviour.

Instead of resorting to rash behaviour due to impatience, remove yourself from the situation, take a break, go for a walk, have something to eat or drink. Practice mindfulness and meditation. A positive outlook towards life rather than finding outright solutions can achieve closure towards many complex problem situations.

Coaching Activity: Developing Patience

Choose a situation where you want to develop patience.

> Are you aware of your feelings & roles in particular situations?
>
> Is there a role frustration displacement or mismatch?

Pause & reflect on alternative ways to manage the feelings & roles.

> Is there a reasonable evaluation as to why the situation occurred?
>
> Can you recognise the triggers of impatience such as anger rush, clenched jaws, irritability & tension?

Try these ways to remain calm.

> Take deep breaths, practice mindful breathing & meditation.
>
> Remove yourself from the situation, take a break and have something to eat & drink.
>
> Remain positive & have a higher sense of purpose.

@VN9ClinicalS / Coaching

5.
RESILIENCE

"MAKE TIME FOR RESILIENCE"

Resilience is a way of coping skills to make yourself stronger and thrive. Developing resilience helps strengthen the mindset to overcome problems & have a positive outlook towards growth.

Reflective practice is an essential part of developing your resilience. Reflective exercises involve being aware, accepting things and acknowledging your emotions and how strong or helpless you were in the situation. What could have been done better by others, and by yourself? How could you have influenced the situation to get another outcome?

Resilience is having the belief and the resourcefulness that you can look at a problem or situation in life with different perspectives and come up with solutions. Resilience gives us strength & stability to recognise the things that we can control and accept the things beyond our control. Making time for resilience enables us to look at situations to spot the silver lining in the clouds.

Developing gratitude towards the things we have is the next part of developing resilience. Gratitude towards what we have may be as simple as being grateful for all the positive, daily things and activities that bring joy in life. Finding time to do more of such activities that bring happiness, comfort and finding your zone to thrive are ways to achieve resilience.

Resilience includes personal characteristics such as adaptability, self belief, situational response, response to challenges and use of support systems.

Tap into your support system of family and friends to explore backing to develop the personal resilience systems.

Resilience is necessary to prevent burnout in job situations and decrease stress levels. Being resilient about problems helps set strategies towards long-term goals in business and management.

These dimensions, such as adaptability of the individual personality, having a positive mindset, developing resilience in the face of the various adversities in life, and emotional intelligence, give the so called "soft skills" necessary for professional and personal growth and development.

Developing Resilience

REFLECTION
What are your emotions about the situation / things?
What could have been done better by you?

PERSPECTIVES
Is there another take on the situation?
Can you spot the 'silver lining in the dark cloud'?

ACCEPTANCE
What are the things you can control?
What is beyond your control & influence?

GRATITUDE
What are the things that you are grateful about in situations?
What are the day-to-day activities that bring joy to your life?

THRIVING ZONE
Can you find the time & support systems to do the activities that you enjoy?
Find your thriving zone

REFLECTION ➡ PERSPECTIVES ➡ ACCEPTANCE ➡ GRATITUDE ➡ THRIVING ZONE

@VN9ClinicalS

HOW TO DEVELOP EMOTIONAL INTELLIGENCE AND RESILIENCE

Activity Sheets

The five coaching activity sheets can be used for emotional intelligence and resilience development for personal use or can be used for EI and resilience training in organisations

Emotional Intelligence

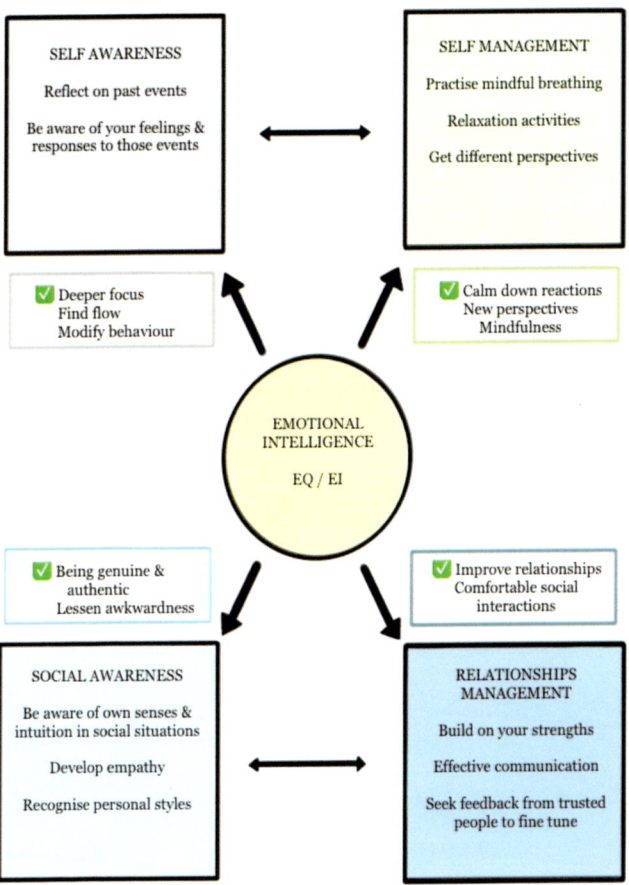

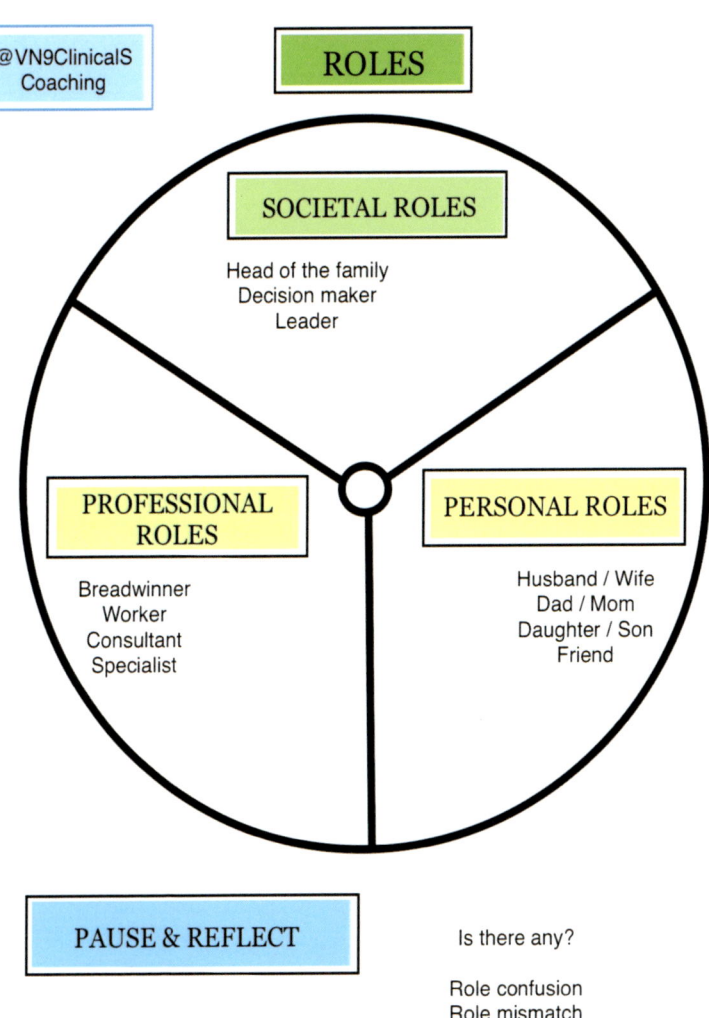

Coaching Activity: Developing Patience

Choose a situation where you want to develop patience.

> Are you aware of your feelings & roles in particular situations?
>
> Is there a role frustration displacement or mismatch?

Pause & reflect on alternative ways to manage the feelings & roles.

> Is there a reasonable evaluation as to why the situation occurred?
>
> Can you recognise the triggers of impatience such as anger rush, clenched jaws, irritability & tension?

Try these ways to remain calm.

> Take deep breaths, practice mindful breathing & meditation.
>
> Remove yourself from the situation, take a break and have something to eat & drink.
>
> Remain positive & have a higher sense of purpose.

@VN9ClinicalS / Coaching

Developing Resilience

REFLECTION

What are your emotions about the situation / things?
What could have been done better by you?

PERSPECTIVES

Is there another take on the situation?
Can you spot the 'silver lining in the dark cloud'?

ACCEPTANCE

What are the things you can control?
What is beyond your control & influence?

GRATITUDE

What are the things that you are grateful about in situations?
What are the day-to-day activities that bring joy to your life?

THRIVING ZONE

Can you find the time & support systems to do the activities that you enjoy?
Find your thriving zone

REFLECTION ➡ PERSPECTIVES ➡ ACCEPTANCE ➡ GRATITUDE ➡ THRIVING ZONE

@VN9ClinicalS

EMOTIONAL INTELLIGENCE COACHING
@ VN9 CLINICAL SERVICES LTD

How to Develop Emotional Intelligence and Resilience

Part of the Coaching Activities Workbook
Audio Podcasts on Spotify.

Listen to the audio version of the book publications by VN9 Clinical Services Ltd:

podcasters.spotify.com/pod/show/vn9clinicals

Developed and Published by
VN9 Clinical Services Ltd

HOW TO DEVELOP EMOTIONAL INTELLIGENCE AND RESILIENCE

ABOUT THE AUTHOR

Dr Veena V Nanjangud
MBBS, Postgraduate Diploma in Business Administration (Open)

Managing Director
VN9 Clinical Services Ltd

VN9ClinicalS.com

The copyrights of the book 'How to develop emotional intelligence and resilience' belong to ©Dr Veena Nanjangud. The contents of this book are intended as a guide and not professional advice. With no liabilities to VN9 Clinical Services Ltd and the author because of the contents and the material in this book.

Milton Keynes UK
Ingram Content Group UK Ltd
UKRC031931280324
440347UK00005B/38